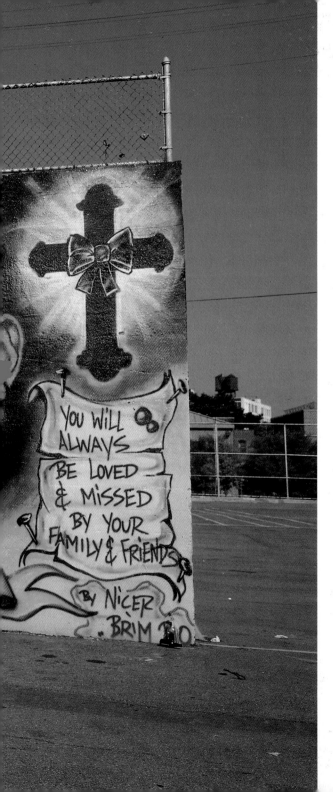

R.I.P.

NEW YORK SPRAYCAN MEMORIALS

MARTHA COOPER • JOSEPH SCIORRA

WITH 137 COLOUR ILLUSTRATIONS

Thames & Hudson

On the title pages: Nicer, Brim, and Bio, *In Memory of Tony*, 1992,
Cypress Avenue and East 141st Street, Mott Haven, Bronx.

First published in the United Kingdom in 1994 by Thames & Hudson Ltd,
181A High Holborn, London WC1V 7QX

www.thamesandhudson.com

© 1994 Thames & Hudson Ltd, London
Photographs © 1994 Martha Cooper
Reprinted 2001

British Library Cataloguing-in-Publication Data
A catalogue record for this book is available from the British Library
ISBN 0-500-27776-1

Printed and bound in Singapore by C.S. Graphics

R.I.P.

NEW YORK SPRAYCAN MEMORIALS

CONTENTS

Memory is triggered by contact with the objects and places associated with past events. This is one reason why so many who choose to remember set off on pilgrimage to battlefields, concentration camps, and Hiroshima's ground zero. We erect monuments at these epicenters of suffering and sorrow in order to appease the voices who demand that we bear witness to their pain and our horror.

In New York, the young Latino and African American men and women who have died and are dying in epidemic proportions in the city's battle-torn streets are commemorated by family and friends who commission artists to create murals on the sides of buildings. Painted memorials continue to mark the site of a tragic death long after newspaper reporters and television camera crews

INTRODUCTION
THE ART OF MEMORIALIZING IN AN AGE OF VIOLENCE

have left the scene. The ongoing violence in the public sphere contributes to an overwhelming despair and necessitates a communal response to help neighborhood residents overcome their bereavement collectively. Memorial walls are reminders of, if not indictments against, civil society's inability or unwillingness to address the systemic poverty and the pervasive racism that promote the rampant flow of drugs and guns into inner-city communities.

Photographer Martha Cooper and I first came across memorial walls in the summer of 1988, the year they burst onto the urban landscape in a spray of vibrant color. Chico's commemorative murals

Jamaal "Rasta" Pete completing the portrait
of U.S. Airforce Sergeant Hector Alvarez,
who died suddenly of a blood clot.

The late graffiti artist, Eugene "Risk" Cleary, appears in Hoist's tribute as a winged spraycan flying to heaven.

on the Lower East Side were the first we noticed by a single artist appearing with any regularity. In time, Chico was joined by, among others, Tracy, Per, Nomad, Caso, Solo, Paco, F-Boom, and members of the TAT crew Nicer, Bio, Brim, and B-GEE 183. We also met artists Dragon, Vonce, and Sammy Zarrilla, who paint exclusively with airbrush. These professional and semi-professional artists, who have mastered their craft and are creating a body of stylistically discernible work, are distinguished from the untrained individual who paints a simple but heartfelt memorial to a close friend. As we talked with the artists about their creations, we became fascinated with this new genre of art born from bloodshed and grief.

Over the next six years we witnessed the memorial wall tradition establish itself in the city in close relationship to the proliferation of handguns and the escalating violence. Time and time again, people we met in Manhattan, Brooklyn, and the Bronx would cite a litany of murals scattered throughout their neighborhood and beyond for the staggering number of people killed in countless street skirmishes. In the fall of 1993, graffiti connoisseur and unofficial historian Francisco "Pops" Rivera took us on a whirlwind tour through northern Brooklyn, expounding on the current state of violence and the merits of different artists' work on seemingly endless walls. The city is at a grievous moment in history when African American and Latino children, anticipating an early death, prepare for its arrival by approaching respected community artists to paint their memorials.

Not all memorials are drug-related or for homicide victims. A mural may be painted for a person killed in a traffic accident or for someone who suffered a fatal illness. Three walls we encountered were for middle-aged Latino men who died of heart attacks. We know of two walls dedicated to men who died of AIDS.

A devotional candle burns eternally anchored in a favorite drink.

It is plausible that a number of deaths attributed to an illness such as asthma may in fact have been complicated by AIDS or drug abuse. In the course of documenting memorial wall art we did not feel compelled to uncover the detailed circumstances leading to the demise of each individual. Family members, friends, and the artists told us how a person died, but were reluctant to discuss the role drug addiction or turf wars may have played in death. It was not our mandate to probe.

This photo of Pupi in happier days is now sealed behind plexiglass and mounted on his memorial.

Driven from the subways by zealous municipal officials and dismissed as passé by international art dealers, graffiti has returned to its roots and reemerged as a viable, vernacular art form. The brick and concrete surfaces of apartment buildings and playgrounds are the preferred contemporary canvases. "Look at the walls," pioneer artist Lady Pink recently exclaimed. "The energy is still there — energy to create, energy to be seen, energy to be heard." All the mainstream media meanwhile continue to treat aerosol art as deviant behavior, devaluing its aesthetic and social contributions.

Graffiti artists currently producing memorials differ in a number of ways from earlier subway writers. Today's muralists are a considerably older group, with the average age being about twenty-five. With exception of Janet Velásquez, who collaborated with Chico on one East Harlem wall, we heard of no other female memorialist. Several artists are academically trained: Jabster, Jad, and Tracy attended

Paco's graveyard scene in Brooklyn's East New York.

A Jewish Star of David for fifteen-year-old Johanna, in a Brooklyn schoolyard.

An Albanian flag on a Bronx memorial.

Manhattan's famed High School of Art and Design. Nomad holds a bachelor's degree from the School of Visual Arts and designs prototypes of commercial packaging. Jabster and others have their own line of clothing. Some artists feature their hip hop fashion and paraphernalia in their own shops, such as Kaves's Brooklyn BMT Line and Síen's On Da Down Low in the Bronx.

Latino artists play a predominant role in the development of the New York memorial tradition, and of these the overwhelming majority are Puerto Ricans. The work of white artists Michael Tracy and Frank Fischetti is found in the Bronx. African American painters Vonce Campbell, Shaabani "Sha-Black" Dekattu, and Jamaal "Rasta" Pete entered the scene in 1993 as we were completing this book.

The strong Latino presence reveals a historic precedent for the memorial tradition. The walls are updated versions of the simple roadside crosses often erected at the site of an automobile accident in predominantly Catholic countries. These wood, metal, and cement crosses manifest the belief that the souls of those who die unexpectedly and fail to receive the Last Rites of the Catholic Church are suffering in purgatory's purifying flames. The marker serves then as a lasting reminder for passersby to pray for the person's soul and thus speed its eventual arrival into heaven.

New York memorial artists were also inspired by the Vietnam Veterans Memorial in Washington, D.C. Unveiled in 1982, the black granite wall is etched with the 58,183 names of the Vietnam War's American casualties. The chevron-shaped monument has been internationally acclaimed for its ability to elicit quiet contemplation on warfare's destructive magnitude rather than champion blind patriotism and macho glory.

R.I.P. Dooza by Brooklyn's Sha-Black.

Detail from Spon and Vulcan's huge wall, Roughneck Reality.

Graffiti's commercial value is another significant component contributing to the emergence of memorial art. During the 1980s, art dealers and gallery owners courted subway writers to create wildstyle pieces on canvas for wealthy collectors. The legitimization of an art form stigmatized as vandalism and the potential profits offered to the artists were particularly seductive at a time when city officials were conducting a successful campaign to eradicate graffiti from subway trains.

As the art world failed to live up to its financial promise, young artists turned to neighborhood businesses offering customized advertisements for a fee. Soon the walls and protective metal gates of grocery stores, religious shops, pizzerias, and automobile repair garages were decorated with fancy lettering and colorful cartoon characters heralding merchandise and services. Chico played a pivotal role in this transition from subway writer to muralist for hire and, finally, to memorial artist. Today, Chico and Per sign contracts to promote the products of international companies such as Coca Cola, Wrangler Jeans, and McDonald's.

New York's memorial art developed in close connection to the indiscriminately violent street battles waged for slivers of the city's lucrative drug trade. Dealers seeking to honor fallen comrades could afford to pay top dollar for a wall, and as a result they helped establish the business of memorial art. While Tracy and Chico have made a conscientious choice not to commemorate drug dealers, others are unwilling to relinquish what they consider to be an advantageous commercial opportunity.

Bart Simpson, decked out in gold chain and hightops, toting a pistol.

The price of a memorial is calculated on a number of variables. Many artists, especially those who knew the deceased, are content simply to create, and only ask to be reimbursed for the paint. Nicer and fellow members of the TAT crew charge according to their relationship to the deceased and the clients' ability to pay. Per refuses to work for what he considers "crackhead prices." He explained, "Business is business. I feel bad that it happened. But you don't go to the funeral parlor and say, 'Hey, look out for us because our loved one has gotten shot.' Come on. This is a business." Vonce Campbell asks a set fee of approximately $500 for a portrait enclosed in a gold ribbon. Hector Guma has a price sheet based on materials and wall footage, e.g., a handpainted acrylic mural, 10 to 15 feet, $600–$800. The $1,500 Chico received for a huge mural in a Bensonhurst playground in Brooklyn was the largest amount of money we have heard paid for a memorial.

Community patronage is paramount. The artist must take into consideration the aesthetic tastes and religious sensibilities of the deceased's friends and family, not those of the graffiti world. Sketches of the piece are produced for customer approval and

An angel for ten-year-old Jessica Guzman by Andre Charles.

input. A client may request changes at any stage of the work. On occasion, there are disagreements between the deceased's close friends and the more conservative parents. Tony Rosario's parents were deeply offended by the image of a gold chain with the figure of St. Lazarus featured in their son's memorial. They believed gold represented avarice. It was replaced with a radiant wood cross.

Many admirers of subway graffiti found the appropriation of city property a particularly

This list of youthful dead on school composition paper includes famous artist Keith Haring.

A wall for Pito by Chico and Janet Velásquez, in East Harlem.

alluring and provocative feature of the art form. Memorial artists, on the other hand, are more inclined to seek permission for coveted wall space. Nicer approaches landlords, building superintendents, and shop owners with his portfolio of photographed murals. He promotes his work as a contribution to the beautification of the block and surrounding neighborhood. Some artists grapple with municipal bureaucracy in order to place and safeguard memorials on handball courts in city parks. A wall is selected because it is near the place where the deceased died, lived, or congregated with buddies.

While they are intended as lasting tributes, memorial murals are susceptible to damage from a number of sources. Weather, pollution, and time are by far the most harmful agents causing walls to chip and fade. Paco provides specific instructions on how to care for a mural, such as washing it with hot water once a month. Memorials painted on temporary walls of abandoned buildings are eventually destroyed when the structure is renovated. Superintendents often whitewash a mural, especially if they were not petitioned beforehand. In some cases, walls are defaced by rival drug dealers who, having killed a person once, attempt to destroy the deceased a second time by obliterating his memory. Cops have ruined murals honoring victims of police brutality. Time and time again, people return to restore or completely redo murals in order to secure the deceased's survival in the collective consciousness.

Pito's wall, defaced.

Flowers and candles for the late Carlos García on his birthday.

The memorial wall transforms personal grief into shared public sentiment by serving as a vehicle for community affiliation and potential empowerment. Covering the expenses for materials and the artist's labor is often a collective endeavor, with neighborhood residents making contributions in memory of one of their own. The murals create new public spaces for community ceremony. Life is celebrated at the walls with parties marking anniversaries and birthdays. These centers of congregation become rallying points for candlelight processions and demonstrations held by community people who march through the streets in opposition to violence, drugs, or police brutality.

These neighborhood billboards are used to elicit critical examination of the root causes and solutions to the daily onslaught against inner-city youth. The Crown Heights Youth Collective in Brooklyn sponsors memorials in an aggressive campaign to cultivate alternatives to violence among the neighborhood's Caribbean and African American kids. Teenage members of the South Bronx Photographic Center, housed in the All Saints Lutheran Parish, used their photo exhibit documenting community life and commemorative murals to kindle discussion on the untimely deaths of neighborhood residents. Memorial walls are designed to stimulate both the heart and the mind, tapping art's transformative and healing powers.

The images in this book represent only a fraction of those we documented; they are a small part of the two thousand plus killings that occur each year in the city. Turn the page and witness a generation of sons and daughters — now gone.

JOSEPH SCIORRA

A street sign is transformed by Tracy into a memorial for the neighborhood.

rawing from sources sacred and profane, memorial artists creatively juxtapose an array of images and symbols in their work. Their innovative mix allows for individual input while establishing the parameters of this recent genre of graffiti art.

A skull's piercing gaze is the most striking representation of death. In Chico's harrowing vision, the death's head is the latest addition to the New York skyline, seen tilting precariously above the city's mounting dead. Artists Nomad and Per once visited a young man's grave in order to reproduce his tombstone accurately on a memorial wall. Some walls include whole rows of tombstones, inscribed with the names of neighborhood youth.

Religious imagery, overwhelmingly Christian, predominates. Crosses, angels, hands clasped in prayer, heaven's clouds, and

IMAGERY

portraits of Christ and the Virgin Mary are among the favorite emblems of faith emblazoned on the urban landscape. Walls containing Islam's Star and Crescent or the Jewish Star of David, although rare, indicate an acceptance of memorial murals beyond their original Catholic Latino audience. Painted candles, flowers, hearts, and other traditional funerary motifs abound.

Muralists strive to capture an individual's personality by taking into consideration the deceased's interests and tastes. A favorite color, a cartoon character, an automobile, or alcoholic beverage not only identifies a specific person but contrasts the stillness of death with the vivacity once exhibited in life. The artist uses these common mass-produced objects to paint a distinctive, symbolic portrait of the memorialized person. *(Antonio "Chico" García, Avenue B, off 12th Street, Lower East Side, Manhattan.)*

IMAGERY

Flowers, hearts, and a softer palette are common features of memorials for women. On Jessica's mural (*left*), Nicer painted over a first attempt at lettering he considered "too guyish." When Jessica's mother balked at plans for her daughter's portrait, Nicer chose a single red rose instead for the 21-year-old, shot by a bullet intended for her boyfriend. *(Hector "Nicer" Nazario, "Bio," Brim, and "B-GEE 183," 1993, Southern Boulevard, off Longwood Avenue, Melrose, Bronx.)*

Millie (*above*) was the fourth memorialized person we heard about who died of asthma, a treatable and readily manageable illness. Ultimately, it was an inadequate health-care system which proved fatal. The eight ball, found on a number of walls, represents either cocaine, a highly desirable brand-name jacket, or the sudden end of the game. Millie loved to play pool. *(Antonio "Chico" García, 1991, Avenue C, off 7th Street, Lower East Side, Manhattan.)*

Per and Nomad adapted this macho image of a suffering Jesus (*above*) from a T-shirt that read, "Lord's Gym/Bench Press This." This memorial was the first in a series of commissioned walls painted on a single block of Boynton Avenue which has become one of the city's many open-air galleries of death and beauty. *(Alfredo "Per" Oyague Jr. and Omar "Nomad" Seneriz, 1993, Soundview, Bronx.)*

Jad plans to redo the mural of Christ he painted for Luis, a neighborhood friend (*right*). It was completed with limited resources — a few spraycans, some house paint, and a couple of messed-up brushes. This sacred portrait adorns a wall adjoining Luis's apartment building. *(José "Jad" Díaz and Carlos "C-Loe" Lebrón, Hooper Street, off South 5th Street, Williamsburg, Brooklyn.)*

Soon after his death in 1992, Albert González's friends commissioned two adjacent but aesthetically different memorials. A graffiti-style piece was designed with the artistic preferences of the neighborhood youth in mind, while this handpainted cross was meant to appeal to an older and more religious audience. *(Artist unknown, Himrod Street, off Myrtle Avenue, Bushwick, Brooklyn.)*

In the early hours of September 9, 1991, a festering argument was revived outside a pool hall and quickly settled with a knife wound that punctured 14-year-old Robert Torres's lung. Robbed of his wallet, the body of "John Doe" lay in the city morgue for a week until his frantic parents finally found him. This mural features a rare representation of God. *José "F-Boom" Crespo and "Dek," Myrtle and Evergreen Avenues, Bushwick, Brooklyn.)*

Popular Catholic iconography provides a well-spring of visual references. Memorial artists borrow images from mass-produced holy cards and religious calendars which they enlarge and incorporate into their public art. Adapted to urban architectural features, these memorials serve as billboards proclaiming an optimistic belief in a rewarded afterlife. (Far left: *Artist unknown, 1992, East 116th Street, off 2nd Avenue, East Harlem, Manhattan.* Left: *Artist unknown, 1992, East 108th Street and 1st Avenue, East Harlem, Manhattan.* Above: *James de la Vega, East 102nd Street, off Park Avenue, East Harlem, Manhattan.*)

The deceased may be remembered by their possessions as well as by their portraits. Evoking the prestige, expensive consumer goods bestowed in life, images such as the red Nova (*above*) identify an individual in the same way as do the iconic attributes of Catholic saints. Cano's killer was AIDS, the number one cause of death for American men aged 25 to 44. (*Antonio "Chico" García, 2nd Street, off Avenue B, Lower East Side, Manhattan.*)

"I paint people's fantasies," Hector Guma told us. In the case of Jorge Fuente, aka Pocho, these included his vehicles of choice. Now the road leads in only one direction. (*Hector Guma, Reyer Avenue, off East 183rd Street, Tremont, Bronx.*)

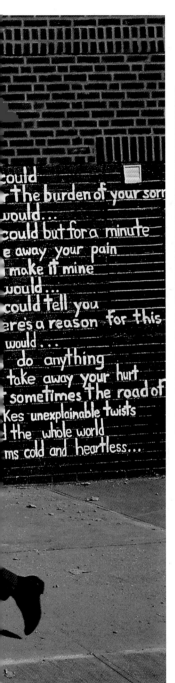

Sal Frisella lost control of his motorcycle on a rainy summer night and, along with companion Damian Volpe, skidded into an oncoming car. Their friend, artist Pascal Di Bello, reproduced the winged rose pierced by a sword from a Billy Joel concert T-shirt which, in turn, was based on traditional biker imagery. The poem was copied from a funeral card. *(Pascal Di Bello, 67th Street, off 18th Avenue, Bensonhurst, Brooklyn.)*

The Ching-a-ling Nomads, a motorcycle gang, created this collective tribute to their fallen comrades. The wall's Satanic and Nazi visual references, typical of motorcycle gangs, stand in stark contrast to the prevailing Christian themes in memorial art. The flames of hell counter the common perception that all are peacefully resting in paradise. *("Cuba," East 180th Street, off Hughes Avenue, Tremont, Bronx.)*

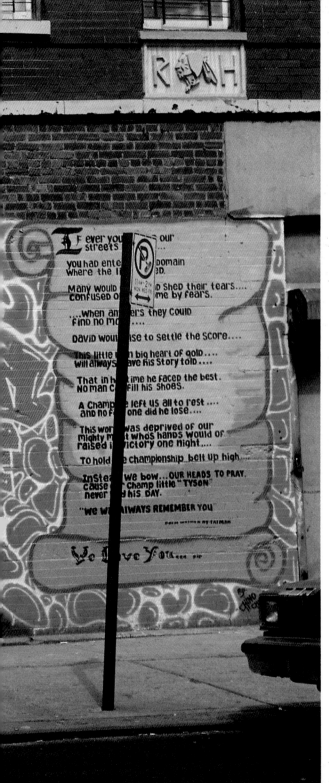

The subjects of these murals, 17-year-old David Rivera and 24-year-old Juan "Tee" Castro, were said to be good with their hands. They were known in East Harlem as street fighters. But in an age when an argument between men is no longer settled with fisticuffs, the gun has the final word. Six years apart but a mere block away from each other, both men were shot dead.

(Left: Raymond "Chino" Rodríguez and Ismael "Peachy" Rivera, poem by "Fat Man," East 119th Street, off 2nd Avenue, East Harlem, Manhattan. Above: Oliver "Caso" Ríos and José "Solo" Cordero, East 118th Street, off 3rd Avenue, East Harlem, Manhattan.)

When two young East Harlem men died in 1993, one from asthma and the other from a gun, friends initiated an annual basketball tournament in their honor. Artist Verse (left) and Ken Bazemore are seen above wearing memorial T-shirts used as uniforms by the opposing teams. *(Juan "Verse" Ayala, East 123rd Street, off 2nd Avenue, East Harlem, Manhattan.)*

Willie, a lover of sports, was slain in the Bronx getting out of his car. "It's a shame," said artist Solo. "Sometimes you see people grow up and you try to look out for them and they take a wrong route. It's just the way things out here is." *(José "Solo" Cordero, In Memory of Willie (detail), 1992, East 117th Street, off 2nd Avenue, East Harlem, Manhattan.)*

Cartoon "characters" were a major source of images for subway graffiti writers in the heyday of the 1980s. These animated stars of television and comic books, who bounce back to life when shot, continue to pop up to pay their respects.

Betty Boop (*right*) was a favorite of 10-year-old Jenny Valentine and 11-year-old Evelyn León, who were crushed beneath a collapsing marble entrance. Chico's memorial decorates a nearby playground created in the tragic aftermath as a safe haven for neighborhood children. *(Antonio "Chico" García, 1988, East 13th Street, off 2nd Avenue, Lower East Side, Manhattan.)*

Michael Tracy's Touché Turtle salutes the late José Luis Soto. A father of three, José was preparing to return to the Bronx after an unsuccessful go of it in Puerto Rico when he was caught in cross-fire. His body was flown back to New York for burial and his memorial painted on the corner where he hung out. *(Michael Tracy, West 190th Street, off University Avenue, University Heights, Bronx.)*

Puerto Rican and father is Indo-Trinidadian, is a popular artist in Upper Manhattan. His depiction of a crucified Dominican flag compares Christ's suffering to that of the immigrant community which has lost many young members to America's killing fields. The artist added his beeper number beneath the flag to attract future clients. *(Darwin "Síen" Bharath,* En Memoria de Richard *(detail), 1993, West 152nd Street, off Broadway, Washington Heights, Manhattan.)*

The huge Puerto Rican flag in this handball court tribute explicitly identifies Johnny Román's death as a collective loss. The 28-year-old was stabbed in a fight in, ironically, Happy Warrior Park. *(William "Bill Blast" Cordero, Amsterdam Avenue and West 98th Street, Upper West Side, Manhattan.)*

IN LOVING MEMORY
OF Johnny

11·29·61   8·12·90

Unlike subway graffiti, the name of the deceased, rather than the artist, is the centerpiece of memorial wall art. The artist's name, if included at all, is of minor significance.

While subway writers painted their tag names in esoteric wildstyle, memorial artists' inscriptions are legible to the general public. Since these murals offer the passerby a station for solace and contemplation, it is important that they be visually accessible.

Community patronage is paramount and friends and family may dictate what is included on a wall. The artist may receive a list of names to inscribe in paint or be told to change a phrase or image the family finds offensive. The words "IN MEMORY OF ...," "REST IN PEACE," and "R.I.P.," or their Spanish equivalents, are standard text and often written on painted ribbons floating above the name. As with tombstones, birth and death dates are listed.

WORDS

The artist is allowed his say in the epitaph written for the deceased, even though the two may never have met. Often another person actually composes the words. Painted in scrolls or open books, the text might extol a person's character or empathize with the family's loss. A brief verse from the scriptures may speak to God's magnitude. Occasionally, the artist/poet comments directly on the injustices and bloodshed of inner-city America. One Upper Manhattan memorial demands, "Stop the Violence!" (*see page 15*).

Vonce Campbell writes the names of those who commissioned this Brooklyn memorial (*left*) to Ben Pérez, 28, who was gunned down in a dance club parking lot. The airbrushed champagne is offered in eternal toast.

As Sheer worked on this memorial (*below*) to a high school student shot during lunch break, neighborhood people approached him about getting their names on the growing list of friends. Since it wasn't the artist's place to add the new names, he appropriately deferred to Javier, who had put up the money for paint. Two weeks later, 18-year-old Javier was fatally shot. (*Orlando "Sheer" Cepeda,* Rest In Peace Juan Luie *(detail), 1993, East 112th Street, off 2nd Avenue, East Harlem, Manhattan.*)

Commentary such as this observation from the urban battlefront recalls the messages graffiti artists once sprayed on subway cars as part of their pieces. (*"Seres" and "Simon,"* In Memory of Fern *(detail), 1993, West 136th Street, off Broadway, Harlem, Manhattan.*)

Right: *Artist unknown*, In Memory of Wally *(detail)*, 1986, East 111th Street, off Lexington Avenue, East Harlem, Manhattan.

Far right: *Artist unknown*, PJ *(detail)*, 1992, Clay Avenue, off East 167th Street, Morrisania, Bronx.

Oliver "Caso" Ríos and José "Solo" Cordero, poem by Julio "Fade" Cabán, The Legend Lives On, Tee *(detail), 1993, East 118th Street, off 3rd Avenue, East Harlem, Manhattan.*

Right: *Artist unknown*, Spoony *(detail)*, 1993, Clay Avenue, off East 167th Street, Morrisania, Bronx.

WALLY 7/7/73
R.
ROQUEL 86

LOVE ... ROB.

Wally Man Full of Happiness

Wally Man full of happiness, Laughter, Love,
For Others Full of Smiles and Kindness
With Friends of Childhood Wally ...
Facing the Problems of Life
and Love Sharing his Love with
Others. Smiling with every day Life
your time has come. But You are
in the Heaven above, Feeling
The warmth of the Sun, Hearing
the Songs of the Angels,
Walking through the green grass and
Flowers of the heaven Memories of
good times and bad will be Remembered
Family, we remember the Smile of
Love which you Shared with all Seeing
From above, the Tears of Love from
the eyes of Family and Friends
They all   Love You

SALE POINT

This Ain't No Playground.

AIR MAX

CONVERSE

WE LOVE YOU PJ RIP

ONE LOVE 16A

BARRY DION
JAMEO TIM SALY
SKI LEE
ALGEE VINNIE
DOG BINGO
BRUICE AL
16V BUTCH
15V BIRDIE
MACK MIKE
BOELO ROC
FAT LARRY
TRAIN MILO
GEE DAP
HAMMED CHAZ
MONTE EDDIE
BIZ BLONDIE
OON STACEY
TY
RACKOBLACK

IN MEMORY OF

ANT   GREG
ALBEE   J.B.
CURTIS   DARNEL
SAL.TDP.   ROX
SLOPE   LONNY
ROLAND   ROCCA
COCOA

REST IN PEACE

Grassroots organizations working to prevent violence in their communities may occasionally sponsor memorials as combined tribute and teaching tool.

St. Peter's-in-the-Bronx Church is a self-described "neighborhood ministry." It brought public scrutiny to the murder of 21-year-old José Luis Ortiz, aka Moondog, by commissioning a memorial and holding a candlelight procession through the troubled streets of the South Bronx. The theme of non-violence reverberates in the celebration of the youth's January 15th birthday, which he shared with civil rights leader Dr. Martin Luther King. *(David Green, poem by Nicole Black Woods, 1989, East 140th Street, off Willis Avenue, Mott Haven, Bronx.)*

The Crown Heights Youth Collective is responsible for several neighborhood memorials, including this one for Police Officer Herman, 24, killed responding to a dispute between two former lovers. According to artist Alan Williams, "We did it because Jeff was a righteous man, a fair man." *(Menelek III, Alan Williams, and Willard Whitlock, Bedford Avenue and Sullivan Place, Crown Heights, Brooklyn.)*

As memorial walls became increasingly common in New York, old-school graffiti artists have taken to dedicating pieces to colleagues, as they occasionally did on subway trains.

In 1993, Doze painted this R.I.P. tribute to Rasean, Bucky 4, Lil' Edgar, Rook, and Kuriaki, former members of the Rock Steady crew which popularized break dancing internationally. The park, unofficially named after the troupe, is where "old school meets new school, the true school." *("Doze," with "West One" and "Zodak," Amsterdam Avenue and West 98th Street, Upper West Side, Manhattan.)*

At the Graffiti Hall of Fame in East Harlem, Bio reserved a space in his contemporary wildstyle burner for the late writer Shy 147. *(Bio, 1993, East 106th Street and Park Avenue, East Harlem, Manhattan.)*

Portraiture has emerged as a key feature distinguishing contemporary memorials from subway art. Graffiti artists who have mastered the technique of spray paint lettering often join forces with talented portraitists in successful creative and business ventures. Dragon specializes exclusively in portraits, leaving the mural background to local artists. A common bristle brush or electric-powered airbrush are the portrait painter's tools of choice. Either of these offers greater control than the spraycan, allowing for a more detailed and defined shaded image.

Portraits range in style from cartoon line drawings to photorealist depictions. The majority are close-ups of faces whose eyes meet the viewer's in a haunting stare. Others smile or wear a menacing scowl. Vonce has created full-body portrayals of young men posing casually, frozen in time.

PORTRAITS

Commissioning the painted likeness of a recently deceased loved one was common in 19th-century America. While then the finished product was based on a posthumous sketch, late-20th-century muralists always work from a photograph. One Brooklyn memorial contains a mounted 8 x 10 color photo sealed behind plexiglass. While practiced in socially disparate eras, both traditions incorporate the painted portrait into the grieving process.

Some family members find it too painful to encounter their loved one's countenance on the street each day and ask that an alternative image be used. But for Liz Rosario, seeing her brother Tony's portrait (*title pages*), which faces her apartment window, is an essential part of coping with death. "To me it's like a sign of life," she said. "It's like having him still around." (*Hector Guma, 1992, Grand Concourse, off East 181st Street, Morris Heights, Bronx.*)

The artistic team of Per and Nomad has made a name for itself in the Bronx by wedding graffiti graphics and art-school naturalism. Their combined talents command prices which have topped the $1,000 mark. Their first memorial portrait was for 22-year-old Red, who was shot five times with a .25 mm. semiautomatic for kicking out a local drug dealer from the family-owned pizzeria. He was slain riding his mountain bike. *(Alfredo "Per" Oyague Jr. and Omar "Nomad" Seneriz, 1993, Morrison and Westchester Avenues, Soundview, Bronx.)*

Seventeen-year-old Noemí "Suly" Villafañe was three months pregnant when a bullet from her boyfriend's gun snuffed out her life. While painting, Per improvised the anti-violence message on the spot in rap-like fashion. *(Boynton Avenue, off Watson Avenue, Soundview, Bronx.)*

Memorial walls often mark the place where a person died.

Angie left her son and mother in their idling car to place a quick call from this telephone at a Bronx gas station. As the 4-year-old released the brake while playing with the gearshift, his panic-stricken grandmother grabbed the steering wheel and accidently put the car into reverse, killing her daughter as she ran screaming into the street. (Antonio "Chico" García, Bruckner Boulevard, off Brook Avenue, Mott Haven, Bronx.)

Chico's first portrait was for JR, a high school friend who was cut down in a hail of bullets from a drive-by shooting near this empty lot. The Lower East Side mural has since been defaced by rival dealers. (Antonio "Chico" García, East 3rd Street, off Avenue D, Lower East Side, Manhattan.)

As the memorial market booms in New York, non-graffiti artists have become increasingly involved in this new category of public art. Dominican-born Sammy Zarrilla is an academy-trained professional sign painter. We caught up with him on Amsterdam Avenue decorating an awning of a laundromat. He held a decisively negative opinion on memorials: "It's not right. Being in public and all. I don't see any value in it. Sure, the colors are pretty. The art's beautiful. But it's not right. I do it because they pay me. Besides, I don't like looking everyday at someone who's dead." (Below: *Sammy Zarrilla, West 163rd Street, off Broadway, Washington Heights, Manhattan.* Right: *Sammy Zarrilla and "Gringo," West 164th Street, off Broadway, Washington Heights, Manhattan.*)

"GO ALL OUT... BENJI"

It's like me giving back to the community."

Although he has never met any of his subjects, Vonce nonetheless has become personally involved: "I interview the families. I have to know what happened, exactly where it happened so I can feel it. And I always save the faces for last. Then I say a prayer and call it a day." *(Far left: Knowledge, Dodworth Street, off Broadway, Bushwick, Brooklyn. Left: Ben, Maujer Street, off Lorimer Street, Williamsburg, Brooklyn. Below: Big Mal, Saratoga Avenue, off St. Marks Avenue, Crown Heights, Brooklyn. Right: Shahid, Throop Avenue, off Myrtle Avenue, Bedford Stuyvesant, Brooklyn.)*

Vonce Campbell burst on the scene in 1993 with these four airbrush portraits painted in different Brooklyn neighborhoods. He has brought a highly developed commercial sense to memorials, charging a fixed fee based on wall footage and imagery. But the approximate $500 he asks for a face and gold ribbon is much less than what he charges for designing logos for rap groups and backdrops for music videos. "These people all get together and chip in to put the mural up," he explained. "That's why the price is kind of low.

EF by Puppet

Red by Nomad

2 Be by
Hector Guma

Plex by Puppet

Mike by Tracy

Angie by Chico

Nie by F-Boom

Green Eyes by
F-Boom and Hops

Tony

Edgar by Poke

Hec Tec by
Tito Ortiz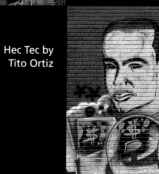

Tee by
Kazo and Solo

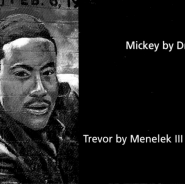

Mickey by Dragon

Trevor by Menelek III

Prince by Tracy

Fern by Simon

Jelvi

The portraits seen here belong to ordinary people and common criminals. There's a poet, a singer, and a United Nations soldier. Their deaths are the result of accident, poor health, and suicide. The overwhelming majority were shot dead in the streets.

It is ironic that mortal enemies peacefully share these pages. Word has it that Hec Tec was executed in retaliation for ordering the murder of 2 Be. At stake was a small piece of the profitable street trade of imported drugs.

Boss by Kaves

Georgie

Bimbo by Chico

Paulie

Modesto by Paco

MODESTO BENITEZ
June 29,1965–April 28,1993

Trevor Campbell (*below*) worked as a counselor for the Crown Heights Youth Collective before travelling to the Sinai Peninsula with a United Nations peacekeeping force. His plane crashed on his way back home to Brooklyn.

Nicer uses up to eighteen colors of spray paint to complete a naturalistic portrait, which includes the face, hair, and immediate background. Rap artist Fat Joe da Gangsta paid all expenses for this handball court memorial (*right*) to his

(Above: *Menelek III, 1991, McKeever Place, off Montgomery Street, Crown Heights, Brooklyn.* Left: *Artist unknown (detail), 1991, West 162nd Street, off Amsterdam Avenue, Washington Heights, Manhattan.*)

friend and afterward reproduced it on the back cover of his debut recording. (*Hector "Nicer" Nazario, "Bio," Brim, and "B-GEE 183," 1992, Trinity Avenue and East 165th Street, Melrose, Bronx.*)

Left: "Poke," West 108th Street, off Amsterdam Avenue, Upper West Side, Manhattan.

Right: Joseph "Jew" Rodríguez and Peter "Cine" Motta, Anthony Avenue, off East Tremont Avenue, Tremont, Bronx.

Queens-based Randall "Dragon" Barquero is highly respected in Upper Manhattan, where he has completed a handful of striking black-and-white portraits. He perfected his airbrush technique in the Greenwich Village clothing store, Unique, where he painted T-shirts and leather jackets for nearly five years.

In the summer of 1992, crowds and cars stopped on Vermeylea Avenue to witness Dragon working on the emerging face of another victim of violence. Electricity for the airbrush generator was provided by a local appliance store.

Two neighborhood artists, Dia and Magnum completed the mural's background.

Every twenty seconds a gun is produced in America, with approximately a million and half currently in the hands of New Yorkers. On average, a person is shot in the city every eighty-eight minutes. In the United States, an estimated 37,000 homicides are committed each year. It's not surprising that military doctors now train for battlefield casualties in ghettos and barrios throughout the country.

America's love of firearms and propensity for violence have been passed on to an increasingly younger generation. Metal detectors stand guard to catch the one in five New York high school students who admit to carrying a weapon. Traumatized children from the city's battle-torn neighborhoods have met to share their experiences with counterparts from Beirut and Medellín.

VIOLENCE

The escalating arms race is attributable to the lucrative drug trade, which offers enterprising young men one of the seemingly few opportunities to beat chronic unemployment and systemic poverty. Teenage "posses" wage street battles with sophisticated firepower in efforts to control the competitive crack market, not unlike their Prohibition-era progenitors. Stray bullets catch innocent bystanders in crowded streets and crash through apartment windows, killing babies as they sleep. Easy money and guns confer respect, which in turn promotes a kiddie culture of escalating death and despair.

Graffiti artists chronicle the senseless destruction of a generation of African American and Latino youth not only in memorial walls but also in vibrant murals depicting anti-drug messages and violent themes. *("Spon" and "Vulcan," Roughneck Reality (detail), 1992, East 106th Street and Park Avenue, East Harlem, Manhattan.)*

Paco portrayed Raheem, 19, as Garfield the Cat, the deceased's favorite cartoon character, wearing his preferred sneakers, and packing his revolver of choice. *(Angel "Paco" Bauta, Riverdale Avenue, off Hinsdale Street, East New York, Brooklyn.)*

Gold chains, a wad of cash, a fancy car, and a 9-mm. semiautomatic: signs of the successful street dealer, flaunted in death as in life. *(Artist unknown (detail), 1992, East 149th Street, off Brook Avenue, Mott Haven, Bronx.)*

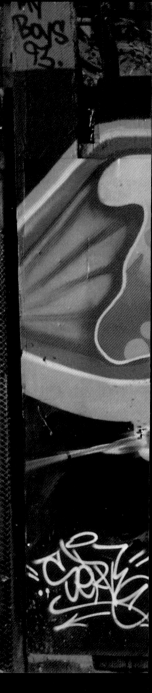

Serve's advertisement for the United Martial Arts School in Parkchester, Bronx (*left*) doubles as an anti-drug mural. The wall, according to the artist, is "a message for kids and people who are scared of drug dealers, who are scared of getting robbed, that they need to fight back." The Chinese characters publicize one of the karate styles taught at the school. *(Joey "Serve" Vega (detail), 1993, Castle Hill Avenue, off Starling Avenue, Parkchester, Bronx.)*

The baby-face, gun-toting characters (*right*) pose as menacing mascots for the defunct "R" automobile club. On Saturday nights, the 300-strong "clan" would drive to the Hunts Point section of the Bronx for drag races. This convoy of cars gave the club its name; the "R" stands for "Rolling Thick." *(Alfredo "Per" Oyague Jr. and Joey "Serve" Vega, Walton Avenue, off East 174th Street, Tremont, Bronx.)*

Spon's specialty is piecing on sanitation trucks. This is his pictorial response to Police Commissioner Raymond Kelly's 1993 decision allowing city cops to carry 9-mm. semiautomatic pistols instead of the standard .38 revolver. Spon explained, "It's a Rest In Peace for the people I know and for the people I don't know that been killed by the police." A few months later, the N.Y.P.D. (New York Police Department) began using military-style, full metal jacket bullets.

Violence also takes the form of an inadequate health care system which fatally discriminates against poor people of color. A man in Bangladesh has a better chance of reaching 65 than an African American male living in Harlem, U.S.A.

Chico painted the image of AIDS dressed in hip hop attire (*above*) after his sister Maria, 30, succumbed to the disease. AIDS is the fourth leading killer of women aged 25 to 44 in the United States. *(Antonio "Chico" García, 1993, Avenue A, off 11th Street, Lower East Side, Manhattan.)*

Artists Per, Nomad, and Serve dubbed the well-dressed crackhead (*right*) "The Judge," as a reminder of the presence of drugs among all social classes. *(Alfredo "Per" Oyague Jr., Omar "Nomad" Seneriz, and Joey "Serve" Vega, 1992, Westchester Avenue, off Fteley Street, Soundview, Bronx.)*

❝We got built-in forgetters," explained Per. The painted memorial attempts to ensure that the tragedy of an individual's death in a violent and indifferent city is not quickly forgotten with yesterday's headlines.

But the urban memorial recalls not only a specific individual but also the circumstances of his or her death. It offers testimony to the violent deaths of Latinos and African Americans brought about by the unchecked proliferation of guns and drugs. The walls are implicit critiques of the social inequities of hard-core poverty, pervasive racism, and official neglect.

A public memorial has the potential to become a focus for concerted action. Neighborhood residents often hold memorial services after the mural's completion. They may reunite there on

REMEMBERING

the anniversary of the person's death or celebrate a birthday at the wall, complete with balloons and cake. Death is answered with the joyous sounds of blaring, thumping, amplified music. Street dancing is offered in celebration of a life as much as in memory of a death.

A tiny gesture is enough to recall a loved one. In the Bronx, Frank Roberts pours a memorial libation for his friend Carlos García each time he opens a bottle of beer, a tradition harkening back to Africa. This personal ritual echoes a line from a Brooklyn mural, "And though you're gone we know you're here, as we twist the cap on every beer." *(Friends of José Luis Soto gather in prayer at a newly completed memorial by Michael Tracy in the Bronx.)*

The art of graffiti serves as street theater for Bertolucci's homeboys, the sponsors of this memorial. The famous Italian film director's name was adopted as street sobriquet by Nuyorican Alberto Silverio, to emulate American mafiosi. *(Hector "Nicer" Nazario, "Bio," and "B-GEE 183," Bruckner Boulevard, off Hoe Avenue, Melrose, Bronx.)*

Millions of Americans celebrate Independence Day each Fourth of July. But for the family of Bangladesh immigrant Angur Hussan, 14, the national holiday also marks the day the boy's throat was sliced by flying metal when members of the Hell's Angels ignited a bag of gunpowder in a garbage can during the motorcycle gang's annual block party. The mural was painted at the site of the tragedy. *("Whiteboy," 1990, East 3rd Street, off 1st Avenue, Lower East Side, Manhattan.)*

The artist Jad stands on the terrace of Carol's apartment building. For him, "The letters have to be really nice because this is for the family. When they come to look at it and to think about the person who died, they don't want to see really deep graffiti because they don't know what it says. It does nothing for them. So you got to make sure that everybody knows what it means. You have to give them the picture." *(José "Jad" Díaz, Bushwick-Hylan Housing, Building 130, 7th floor, Humboldt and Moore Streets, Williamsburg, Brooklyn.)*

A memorial wall does not guarantee one a place in the collective memory. This mural (*above*) was erased a year after we first saw it. When we inquired about the artist, we were told he had left the neighborhood. Even the dry-cleaning place has a new sign and a new owner who never heard of a woman called Sugar. (*"Atom," 1992, Hewes Street, off South 5th Street, Williamsburg, Brooklyn.*)

Raze always wanted to do a wildstyle burner. But as the junior member of the graffiti crew MOM, he never acquired the technique needed to fulfill his dream. Partners Caso and Solo honored him with this memorial burner (*right*). (*Oliver "Caso" Ríos and José "Solo" Cordero, 1993, 3rd Avenue, off East 119th Street, East Harlem, Manhattan.*)

Bronx

Bronx

Bronx

Some homicides gain city-wide and occasionally international notoriety. When African American teenager Yusuf Hawkins (*left*) was shot by a gang of white youths in the streets of Bensonhurst, Brooklyn in 1989, the public outrage shaped that year's mayoral election and provided the inspiration for Spike Lee's film *Jungle Fever*. (*Artist unknown, 1991, Verona Place, off Fulton Avenue, Bedford Stuyvesant, Brooklyn.*)

Muralist Frank Fischetti was one of millions of New Yorkers who came to know Jessica Guzmán from newspaper accounts of her family's desperate search for their only daughter. After her suffocated body was found three days before her eleventh birthday, Fischetti painted this tribute (*left*) because, in his words, "it was the right thing to do." (*Frank Fischetti, 1990, Ellis Avenue, off Castle Hill Avenue, Castle Hill, Bronx.*)

Bronx

Brooklyn

Lives lost are remembered in many ways. We found many quickly assembled altars and simple paintings scattered throughout the city that were no less heartfelt than more elaborate memorials.

Manhattan

Manhattan

Manhattan

Brooklyn

Manhattan

85

The rubbery buildings evoke the surrounding neighborhood where singer George Ortiz grew up (*left*); the circular characters recall his fancy for M&M candy. Jabster and Vinz took six days to complete the mural, and in the process, became close friends with their clients, whom they had previously never met. *(Kenny "Jabster" Rivera and Vincent "Vinz" Sanquiche, Leland and Archer Avenues, Parkchester, Bronx.)*

According to Damaris Lucas, her brother-in-law José "Pochie" Rodríguez, 17, was shot four times in the head over the moneymaking "spot" that is the corner of Grant and East Burnside Avenues in the Bronx. "At first, I used to get sad," she told us. "Now, I get a smile on my face. I don't think about the way he died. I just think about the good memories." *(Alfredo "Kingbee" Bennett, Davidson Avenue, off West Burnside Avenue, Tremont, Bronx.)*

Respected poet, actor, and community activist Bimbo Rivas (*left*) was synonymous with the Lower East Side. He is credited by many for popularizing the Spanish pronunciation of his neighborhood's name, Loisaida. Community residents turned Chico's homage into a poster for a local street fair. (*Antonio "Chico" García, 1992, Avenue C, off 3rd Street, Lower East Side, Manhattan.*)

Residents of Park Place in the Crown Heights section of Brooklyn lit candles to the area's youth honored in Yokonon Israel's 1992 communal memorial (*below*).

The friends of Antonio Gómez celebrated his life as a DJ by using his sound equipment for a party held on the second anniversary of his death (*left*). Victor Rodríguez, aka DJ Craze, operated the turntables for the crowd that gathered to remember their friend through music and dance. Artist Paco (second from left) has painted a dozen memorials in his Brooklyn neighborhood. *(Angel "Paco" Bauta, Hinsdale Street, off Newport Street, East New York, Brooklyn.)*

This rare memorial on canvas (*right*) has been used in anniversary vigils and block parties commemorating the death of Shona Bailey, who was slain as she entered her apartment building. Members of Shona's Girl Scout troop hold up the painting in their meeting space in Harlem's Riverside Community Park Housing. *(Joe "Ezo" Wippler, 1991.)*

Candles illuminate an altar and shrine which were erected on the first anniversary of Jorge Nogue's death at age 27 from a bullet to the neck. *(Luis "Point Zero" Rodríguez, Walton Avenue, off East 183rd Street, University Heights, Bronx.)*

The trio of painted candles (*above*) burning brightly with perpetual flames is a reminder of the living who remember the deceased in prayer. *(Artist unknown, 1992, East 167th Street, off Findlay Avenue, Morrisania, Bronx.)*

In 1993, after five years, the faded and peeling memorial to Eusebio Guzmán (*above*) was replaced with a new one. Cheíto, as he was known to his friends, was sixteen when a city bus struck him as he rode his bicycle a few blocks from home.

Employing a common motif, Per painted the boy's name bursting through a simulated stone wall, forcing Cheíto's memory back into our consciousness. Per copied Cheíto's own words, which the youth had written in the family Bible, onto the wall's upper corner. When the mural was completed, a block party was held on St. Lawrence Street, Bronx, in accordance with the teenager's wish to be remembered with "happiness and laughter."

A neighborhood store donated refreshments and a DJ offered his services for free. In keeping with Puerto Rican tradition, *plena* musicians honored the late Cheíto with songs composed specifically for the event. Seen dancing here, the boy's mother Ely Santiago, who still lives in the apartment above the mural, later confided sadly, "I'm like a clown whose real feelings are hidden from view."